THE LACAYO INSTABILITY INDEX
ECONOMIC STABILITY AND LEADERSHIP 1953-2019

BY

MAX L. LACAYO

Library of Congress Control Number: 2015901909
CreateSpace Independent Publishing Platform, North
Charleston, SC

Lacayo, Max L.
The Lacayo Instability Index / Max L. Lacayo
–2nd ed.–USA
24 p.

ISBN-13: 978-1507826522
ISBN-10: 1507826524

1. ECONOMICS / MACROECONOMICS
2. ECONOMIC INDICATOR

USA, 2015, 2020
Economic Indicator
Second Edition
Printed in USA
Cover design by Max L. Lacayo

THE LACAYO INSTABILITY INDEX
ECONOMIC STABILITY AND LEADERSHIP 1953-2019

MAX L. LACAYO

Sustained economic progress and advances in civilization result, fundamentally, from the interest, effort, freedom and opportunity of individuals to legally acquire private property (land and capital) and accumulate wealth. Private property rights –the precondition of all economic progress– gives the individual security and self-worth. Hence, the individual's rational inclination or incentive to combine labor, capital, land and entrepreneurship to produce wealth and accumulate the physical, human, and intellectual capital necessary to make continuing economic progress possible. In other words, given the opportunities to lawfully acquire property and the freedom to accumulate wealth, the individual is motivated to create, to innovate, to produce the goods and services demanded by society, to trade them and earn a profit. That is how we have come to understand the connection between economic freedom and economic growth, and to value the crucial importance of private property rights.

Within a positive environment of institutional stability and technological advances, the degree of individual willingness and abilities is what ultimately facilitates the more productive use of economic resources and the accumulation of capital necessary for future economic growth. A problem arises, however, when morality of behavior, social concerns, and the basic elements of justice are increasingly ignored by the individual in the market place. In other words, it is not the selfish interest, greed or the individual desire for pleasure what creates progress. A society that grants absolute individual freedom on the sole basis of selfish motives would only promote an unsustainable system of overly concentrated capital, monopolies, exploitation, corruption and social polarization. Progress is not, either, the result of man's natural desire to work hard or of man's concern for his fellow countryman or for mankind. A society that plans solely on those premises is doom to economic disaster or ends up coercing their population to increase the level of production.

It is, then, the degree to which society succeeds in establishing its rules and values what promotes and molds individual actions toward the fulfillments of the desire to own private property and accumulate capital. The more equitable the individual opportunities, the greater are the chances of an individual to compete in the market place. This competition tends to foster innovation, to generate higher levels of productivity, higher profits, more investment, more employment and greater national wealth. Societies that only grant individual freedom and opportunities to a particular sector of the population and invest little or inefficiently in human capital, become dual societies. On one side, a sector develops and progresses until the other sector, which operates at a subsistence level becomes fatigued, unproductive and powerless to sustain the necessary levels of production, income and development. These conditions drag the entire society into the cycle of social unrest that we often see in poor countries.

The most prosperous nations, therefore, are those that can strike a better balance between individual betterment and the social good, prosperity and justice, freedom and order.

Some believe that the natural laws alone explain that the balance of social forces is achieved based on natural conditions such as respect of property rights, good faith, fair transactions and equitable rewards for individual efforts. But the fact is that the economic system cannot be left entirely to self-correcting natural laws, simply because the respect for ownership, sincerity of intention, fairness and the correspondence between individual efforts and rewards are not necessarily natural conditions; at least no more than selfishness, greed, exploitation and corruption.

It is true that individuals are the essential elements of society and that self-interest (motivated by financial compensation, realization, reputation or power) is the driving force of the economy, but the limitations in human capital investment as well as other factors play a significant role on the pattern of income distribution. Since aggregate demand depends on the pattern of income distribution, and production is governed by the pattern of consumer demand, then abnormally unequal income distribution would constrain the level of production and with it the wealth of the nation.

Furthermore, when the private ownership of land and capital is overly concentrated, the economic incentives necessary for economic progress are drastically reduced. This extreme concentration of wealth in the hands of individuals and institutional investors tends to drift away from the production of goods and services as they search for speculative gains. Therefore, to a point, the less polarized the distribution of income, the greater the likelihood of individuals, not only to increase consumption, but also to develop entrepreneurial abilities and increase the competitiveness of the markets.

Economic policies, to be sufficient, should comprehensively support the private sector in the implementation of health, education and training programs, aimed at increasing workers productivity and business profits. The resulting increase in income, savings, and widespread capital accumulation would tend to increase consumption, production and employment. This would allow the economy to utilize more fully its human and capital resources.

Government revenues would also increase, creating more favorable financial conditions, as interest rates would tend to ease. This would allow for higher levels of investment in capital and would help sustain productivity and profits. The high levels of productivity would tend to keep inflation in check.

The most relevant implication here is that governments should promote a more comprehensive and proactive approach to maintain economic freedom, equality of opportunities (not equality of outcomes), growth, and stability, while causing the economic fluctuations (business cycles) to be benign and making fine-tuning government efforts of relatively lesser need.

Virtually, the government primary function is that of stabilizing the economy through monetary and fiscal policies. The idea of success, however, is rather narrow as it concentrates, almost entirely, in the "two unhappy possibilities": the painful reality of inflation and the miserable alternative of unemployment.

Monetary and fiscal policies, if viewed in isolation and as short run instruments of stabilization could at times produce the most unintended results. For instance, massive tax cuts, despite the intention, if disproportionate, could produce an extremely high concentration of capital. Extreme fine-tuning efforts through monetary policy could be deceptive and at times both policies could be contradictory.

Government policies, in general, could be conflicting. One example of the contradictory forces in the United States could be seen in the housing market. At the outset of the XXI century: The government began to expand its social commitment to increase the home ownership of minority groups, while relaxing the accountability of financial institutions. Soon, the real estate industry took advantage of the laissez-faire environment and set itself to put any kind of deals together. Unscrupulous lenders provided the funds so anybody could buy homes, regardless of their credit qualification; they just passed the risk along, selling loans at a profit to third party investors. Borrowers took out loans at low teaser rates, which they could not afford once these low rates expired and their mortgage payments were in many cases doubled. Scores of lending institutions failed, including the giants Fannie Mae and Freddie Mac; leading to a grim credit crunch.

Another important factor, which contributed to the crash of the real estate market, is the role of the speculator. The speculator, attracted by the real estate boom made immense amount of money in their early investments, then dumping in the market their properties at losses they could afford due to their earlier successes but leaving homeowner with houses that were worth less than their mortgage.

This leads us back to the issue of utter concentration of capital. The ideological principle of income polarization has diverted investment from the production of goods and services into speculative investments, which eventually and inevitably lead to markets failure. For a while, the U.S. economic policies have tended to favor the highest income earners. This produced a high concentration of capital that was increasingly channeled into the financial markets in search of capital gains. This speculative investment, which elevated stock prices to unsustainable levels, bears the brunt of the responsibility for the 2008 stock market crash. That situation led to lower capacity to consume due to lower real income and layoffs. That spiral continued to sink the system rapidly, deepening the recession that started in 2007. The U.S. central bank, with the hope of stabilizing the economy, kept lowering the interest rate until it almost reached a near zero level. But, as they say: "you can take a horse to water, but you can't make him drink". Banks kept hoarding cash and not taking the risk of lending it.

On the one hand, the U.S. government treated that economic condition as if it was a short-term imbalance. The reality is that, systematically, middle class families were descending into poverty; many continued to add to the lines of the unemployed or underemployed. Numerous factories closed. The government capacity to continue borrowing money grew impaired. On the other hand, many industries were slapped with excessive regulations that literarily brought them down to their knees. The long-term instability became critical. The trend was signaling that the system could lose its capacity for future prominence.

It is essential, then, that both short and long-term instability be measured and monitored in a practical, straightforward fashion. For that purpose I devised The Lacayo Instability Index, which focuses on four interrelated macroeconomic variables that measure the extent of economic activity, serve as indicators of the health of the U.S. economy, and signal the trend and effect of stabilization policies. This index combines the measurements of inflation (I)[1], twice the value of unemployment (U)[2], the federal deficit as a percentage of GDP (FD%GDP)[3], and a measure of the real GDP drop rate (GDPDR)[4]. The value of unemployment has been doubly weighted due of its impact on the well-being of individuals. Unemployment is not just an unhappy experience; it represents insufferable misery. Economics professor David G. Blanchflower, et al. (2013), presented the results of their economic research in Europe on "the effects of macroeconomic shocks on well-being" at a conference held by the Federal Reserve Bank of Boston. They concluded that unemployment makes people more miserable than inflation. "A 1 percent point increase in unemployment lower well-being nearly four times more than an equivalent rise in inflation," they say. "In Germany, Austria, France and Finland, the elasticity rises to over six times," they added. Justin Wolfers (2003), an economist at the University of Michigan reached a similar conclusion in the United States. The Lacayo Instability Index depicted in EXHIBIT I is the sum of these components:

LACAYO INSTABILITY INDEX= I+U+U+FD%GDP+GDPDR

The use of these variables finds its logic in the rationale that they are, ultimately, the consequences of fiscal and monetary policies, as well as the effects of other aspects of public governance. And in turn, the causes of such public administration efforts are often reflected in the political leaders' adherence to ideological principles, in their attitude toward accountability and their willingness to submit to morality of behavior, to social concerns and to the basic elements of justice.

Exhibit I shows the Lacayo Instability Index of the last 68 years for the United States of America.

For the government to achieve short and long-term stability it would have to implement economic policies that would oppose monopolistic power in all its forms and stimulate competitive markets; it would have to discourage speculative investment and promote productive capital investment; it would have to foster equality of opportunity (not equality of outcome) of individuals to legally acquire private property (land and capital) and to accumulate wealth. The government would have to concentrate on fiscal responsibility and establish reasonable budget-balancing objectives to avoid negative pressures in the financial markets that could result in higher long-term interest rates. It would have to strive to increase exports to avoid unhealthy trade deficits with certain countries and regions; leading to comparative advantages, higher GDP, higher tax revenues, lower Public Debt, and sustained lower unemployment. The Instability Index would allow us to measure and monitor government performance in specific areas needed to sustain economic growth and stability.

The table in exhibit I shows to what extent the policies of each president affect the values of the five components (columns 2 to 6) of the index. The 7th column depicts the sum of these components; the annual value of the index. Column 8 depicts the average of the instability index for the number of years a president has served during an ongoing presidency or during continuous, fully completed, elected terms (i.e. a total of 4 years or a total of 8 years combined as one presidency). Presidencies where the elected president was unable to complete his term are not combined with previous or subsequent terms and are identified as a four-year presidency presided (as if by one president) by the combined name of the president elected and his nonelected successor (see Kennedy/Johnson 4-year presidency and Nixon/Ford 4-year presidency). The Lacayo Instability Index helps judge the president on how he manages what he receives, how he exacerbates or reverses the economic trends and what his long-term economic legacy is. As the index value increases, it indicates that a president execution in terms of economic instability is worsening. **THIS INDEX IS VIRTUALLY A PUBLIC REPORT CARD ON THE PRESIDENTS' SHORT AND LONG-TERM ECONOMIC STABILIZATION ACCOMPLISHMENT.**

The 9th column of exhibit I shows the scores assigned to each president. Such scores are based on the average of the index during the years served by each of the last 12 presidents of the United States subtracted from the average value of the index corresponding to the years served by the previous president. In other words, the higher the score, the better the performance of a president as it compares to the previous president. Of those 12 presidents, Donald Trump and Bill Clinton received the highest positive scores for their efforts toward economic stabilization.

The last, or 10th column shows the ranking of the presidents. President Trump, an economist with a promissory outlook on the American economy, ranks #1. That ranking corresponds to the highest score on the 9th column. President Clinton, ranks #2... and so on.

What is also clear in exhibit I is the accelerated decline of certain long-term economic trends in the United States: the amassing of a colossal public debt and a very unstable approach to fiscal and monetary policy with its consequent long-term instability in the rates of inflation and unemployment. Perhaps political ideology gets in the way of economic performance. Perhaps economic goals are narrowly established due to political pressures. Perhaps politicians fall in love with a tree and ignore the forest. Whatever the reason, it needs to be realized that a piecemeal approach to economic problems is often damaging. The economic reality of a country requires a comprehensive approach and the simultaneous monitoring of a relevant Instability Index and the tendency of its components.

To restore the long-term instability depicted by The Lacayo Index, future U.S. presidents must perform systematically better (lower index values) than their predecessors.

In EXHIBIT II we chart the Instability Index for a 68-year period (1953-2019). We depict the periods of U.S. recessions (dark bars), which are consistent with increasing index levels. On this chart we also mark four economic expansions; the four longest economic expansions in U.S. history, which coincide with periods of decreasing values of the

Instability Index. In EXHIBIT III we chart the performance and ranking of the U.S. presidents during the same period.

We cannot conclude, however, that sporadic drops in the index value would increase long-term economic stability and sustain longer periods of economic expansions. An administration could slash taxes and the Fed could cut interest rates to stimulate economic growth and reduce unemployment, but these could perfectly well reduce the relative value of the Instability Index while leaving unattended the long-term consequences of deficient economic policies. So, the goal of the government should not only aim at obtaining relative declines of the index value, but to maintain the Lacayo Instability Index low in absolute terms while monitoring the level of each of its components.

The problem with economic instability is that the deeper causes of recessions are ignored. We know that at times government itself has been the cause of recessions by applying contractionary fiscal or monetary policies, as they fear inflation. A prevailing traditional assumption –as we enter a recession– is that consumer confidence is down and that a small tax rebate will do the trick and will get the flow of money restarted. At times the government has fought recessions characterized by stagflation by first fighting the inflationary problem with contractionary policies and then reducing taxes regressively to lower businesses costs with the hope of the benefits trickling down to the labor force. But the deeper, more ingrained causes of long-term instability, like profound federal deficits, extreme economic polarization, monopoly power, and the disruptive capacity of rampant speculation are hardly ever addressed.

The complexity of the financial crisis and economic recession that begun in 2007 –the worst since the great depression– is such that left politicians and economists alike, puzzled. This crisis still occupies intelligent minds in the effort of deciphering what went wrong. We know, however, that institutions failed and that society compromised its rules and values. The SEC allowed the proliferation of investors' traps. The Fed, to a large degree, compromised its capacity to stabilize the economy through monetary policy. The permissive monopolistic power granted to certain industries virtually taxed the consumers in detriment of their purchasing power. The play of ideological forces in the branches of government essentially shifted productive capital investment to speculative investment. So bad, that the system virtually shifted from capitalism to what I elected to call *wagerism*.

Since the 1980s, in the United States, money has been gushing to the more affluent members of society and to institutional investors. This degree of wealth concentration has not led to an equally impressive economic growth. Instead, it has produced a decline in real lower and middle incomes. Under these circumstances, consumer demand is often depressed; investment is increasingly drifting away from the production of goods and services and channeled into the speculative search of capital gains. There is little incentive for many wealthy investors to go through the complexities of planning, organizing, directing and controlling a business that produces goods and services when they could profitably bet in the rising prices of stocks, bonds, commodities, etc. and only pay a fraction of the taxes they otherwise would.

High stock prices or the high prices in any speculative market tend to be pushed further upward by astutely fabricated high expectations. In this sense, economic reality and speculative markets are unrelated. *Wagerism* is characterized by the culture of speculation and is an unstable system that inevitably crashes (bubble bursts) after every period of artificially inflated expectations and gains. Another characteristic of *wagerism* is the increasing economic polarization that it imprints in a society. The persistent decline in consumer spending and capital investment, the rising underemployment and income polarization, and the trade imbalances push the system into deeper and more somber tides of speculation.

The great recession that started in December 2007 is clearly marked by the effects of *wagerism*. The modest recovery that started in July 2009 was plagued with escalating joblessness, underemployment, bankruptcies, foreclosures and the risk of inflation. The Fed, starting in 2009, channeled trillions of new dollars into the economy to rescue the failing speculating companies which it deemed "too large to fail." Domestic and foreign banks, hedge funds, mutual funds, large manufacturers, automakers, insurance companies received the bulk of the money distributed as part of the improvised bailout efforts of the Fed.

Amidst our economic uncertainties, one thing is patent: The importance of recognizing the need to embrace a comprehensive economic instability indicator that could help establish a stable long-term path. To avoid further failures and human anguish, the U.S. economy should start producing vigorous increases in real GDP with the minimum possible impact on the public debt. Efforts should be aimed at restoring the size of the middle class instead of allowing monopolies to set arbitrary prices, charge fraudulent fees and outrageous interests while confiscating the purchasing power of consumers. Public policies should be adjusted and laws should be reformed to reduce the substitution of capital investment for speculative investment, to reduce wasteful spending and balance the budget, to promote export-boosting enterprises, to reduce unemployment, to increase productivity and keep inflationary pressures and the interest rates in check.

In all fairness, the Trump administration, which has just completed the first 3 years of its first term, has positioned itself to succeed by creating private investment incentives, discouraging monopolistic behavior, protecting the labor markets, negotiating more favorable international trade deals, lifting detrimental regulatory burdens from businesses, etc. The first phase of President Trump's policies has shown preliminary promising results during the period 2017-2019.

In the subsequent phases of President Trump's governance it is expected an even healthier performance with regard to the GDP, as a result of what he had already set in motion. It is expected, however, a much closer look at the federal deficit, to secure a long lasting positive shock in the economy.

It is opportune, then, to be concerned and more informed –at the public level– about the realities of severe economic fluctuations and to be aware and receptive of practical, comprehensible instruments of analysis and preparedness to gain more wisdom with regard to our selection and election of politicians and to ameliorate the worries about our ability to deal with the next descending economic trend, its untested and costly cures and the capacity of capitalism to endure.

1. INFLATION RATE
DATA SOURCE: U.S. Department of Labor: Bureau of Labor Statistics

2. UNEMPLOYMENT RATE
DATA SOURCE: U.S. Department of Labor: Bureau of Labor Statistics

3. FEDERAL DEFICIT AS A PERCENTAGE OF GDP
FDPGDP = (Federal Deficit / GDP)
DATA SOURCE: Federal Reserve Bank of St. Louis, The White House: Office of Management and Budget

4. REAL GROSS DOMESTIC PRODUCT DROP RATE
GDPDR = - (Real Gross Domestic Product Year 2 - Real Gross Domestic Product Year 1 / Real Gross Domestic Product Year 1) 100
DATA SOURCE: U.S. Department of Commerce: Bureau of Economic Analysis

EXHIBIT I

THE LACAYO INSTABILITY INDEX TABLE 1953-2019 — EXHIBIT I

YEAR	I INFLATION	U UNEMP'MENT	U UNEMP'MENT	FD%GDP FED. DEFICIT	GDPDR GDP DROP RT.	TOTALS INST. INDEX	INDEX AVG. YRS. SERVED	SCORES SUBST. AVGS.	RANK
1953	0.80	2.90	2.90	1.67	-4.688	3.582	EISENHOWER		8
1954	0.70	5.50	5.50	0.30	0.579	12.579			
1955	-0.40	4.40	4.40	0.70	-7.134	1.966			
1956	1.50	4.10	4.10	-0.87	-2.132	6.698			
1957	3.30	4.30	4.30	-0.72	-2.104	9.076			
1958	2.80	6.80	6.80	0.58	0.738	17.718			
1959	0.70	5.50	5.50	2.46	-6.938	7.222			
1960	1.70	5.50	5.50	-0.06	-2.574	10.066	8.613	-2.592	
1961	1.00	6.70	6.70	0.59	-2.561	12.429	KENNEDY/		6
1962	1.00	5.50	5.50	1.18	-6.128	7.052	JOHNSON		
1963	1.30	5.70	5.70	0.75	-4.354	9.096			
1964	1.30	5.20	5.20	0.86	-5.763	6.797	8.844	-0.230	
1965	1.60	4.50	4.50	0.19	-6.498	4.292	JOHNSON		3
1966	2.90	3.80	3.80	0.45	-6.596	4.354			
1967	3.10	3.80	3.80	1.00	-2.742	8.958			
1968	4.20	3.60	3.60	2.67	-4.915	9.155	6.690	2.154	
1969	5.50	3.50	3.50	-0.32	-3.126	9.054	NIXON		10
1970	5.70	4.90	4.90	0.26	-0.186	15.574			
1971	4.40	5.90	5.90	1.98	-3.292	14.888			
1972	3.20	5.60	5.60	1.83	-5.260	10.970	12.622	-5.932	
1973	6.20	4.90	4.90	1.05	-5.645	11.405	NIXON/FORD		12
1974	11.00	5.60	5.60	0.39	0.540	23.130			
1975	9.10	8.50	8.50	3.16	0.207	29.467			
1976	5.80	7.70	7.70	3.94	-5.389	19.751	20.938	-8.317	
1977	6.50	7.10	7.10	2.58	-4.624	18.656	CARTER		7
1978	7.60	6.10	6.10	2.52	-5.535	16.785			
1979	11.30	5.80	5.80	1.55	-3.167	21.283			
1980	13.50	7.10	7.10	2.58	0.257	30.537	21.815	-0.877	
1981	10.30	7.60	7.60	2.46	-2.537	25.423	REAGAN		5
1982	6.20	9.70	9.70	3.83	1.802	31.232			
1983	3.20	9.60	9.60	5.72	-4.583	23.537			
1984	4.30	7.50	7.50	4.59	-7.237	16.653			
1985	3.60	7.20	7.20	4.89	-4.170	18.720			
1986	1.90	7.00	7.00	4.83	-3.462	17.268			
1987	3.60	6.20	6.20	3.08	-3.460	15.620			
1988	4.10	5.50	5.50	2.96	-4.177	13.883	20.292	1.523	
1989	4.80	5.30	5.30	2.71	-3.672	14.438	BUSH		4
1990	5.40	5.60	5.60	3.71	-1.886	18.424			
1991	4.20	6.90	6.90	4.37	0.108	22.478			
1992	3.00	7.50	7.50	4.45	-3.522	18.928	18.567	1.725	
1993	3.00	6.90	6.90	3.72	-2.753	17.767	CLINTON		2
1994	2.60	6.10	6.10	2.79	-4.029	13.561			
1995	2.80	5.60	5.60	2.15	-2.684	13.466			
1996	3.00	5.40	5.40	1.33	-3.773	11.357			
1997	2.30	4.90	4.90	0.26	-4.446	7.914			
1998	1.60	4.50	4.50	-0.76	-4.482	5.358			
1999	2.20	4.20	4.20	-1.30	-4.753	4.547			
2000	3.40	4.00	4.00	-2.30	-4.128	4.972	9.868	8.699	
2001	2.80	4.70	4.70	-1.21	-0.998	9.992	BUSH		9
2002	1.60	5.80	5.80	1.44	-1.742	12.898			
2003	2.30	6.00	6.00	3.30	-2.861	14.739			
2004	2.70	5.50	5.50	3.38	-3.799	13.281			
2005	3.40	5.10	5.10	2.44	-3.513	12.527			
2006	3.20	4.60	4.60	1.80	-2.855	11.345			
2007	2.80	4.60	4.60	1.11	-1.876	11.234			
2008	3.80	5.80	5.80	3.12	0.136	18.656	13.084	-3.216	
2009	-0.40	9.30	9.30	9.78	2.537	30.517	OBAMA		11
2010	1.60	9.60	9.60	8.63	-2.564	26.866			
2011	3.20	8.90	8.90	8.36	-1.551	27.809			
2012	2.10	8.10	8.10	6.65	-2.249	22.701			
2013	1.50	7.40	7.40	4.05	-1.842	18.508			
2014	1.60	6.20	6.20	2.77	-2.526	14.244			
2015	0.10	5.30	5.30	2.43	-2.908	10.222			
2016	1.30	4.90	4.90	3.12	-1.638	12.582	20.431	-7.347	
2017	2.10	4.40	4.40	3.41	-2.370	11.940	TRUMP		1
2018	2.40	3.90	3.90	3.79	-2.927	11.063			
2019	1.80	3.70	3.70	4.59	-2.330	11.460	11.488	8.943	

THE LACAYO INSTABILITY INDEX is a most needed tool to monitor long-term economic tendencies. It combines the measurements of inflation (I), unemployment (U) (twice), federal deficit as a percentage of GDP (FD%GDP), and a measure of the GDP drop rate (GDPDR). The Instability Index is the sum of these components:

$$\text{THE LACAYO INSTABILITY INDEX} = I + U + FD\%GDP + GDPDR$$

EXHIBIT II

EXHIBIT II

THE LACAYO INSTABILITY INDEX (1953-2019)

Increasing values of the index suggest that the instability of the system is increasing. Black bars indicate periods of U.S. recessions.

EXHIBIT III

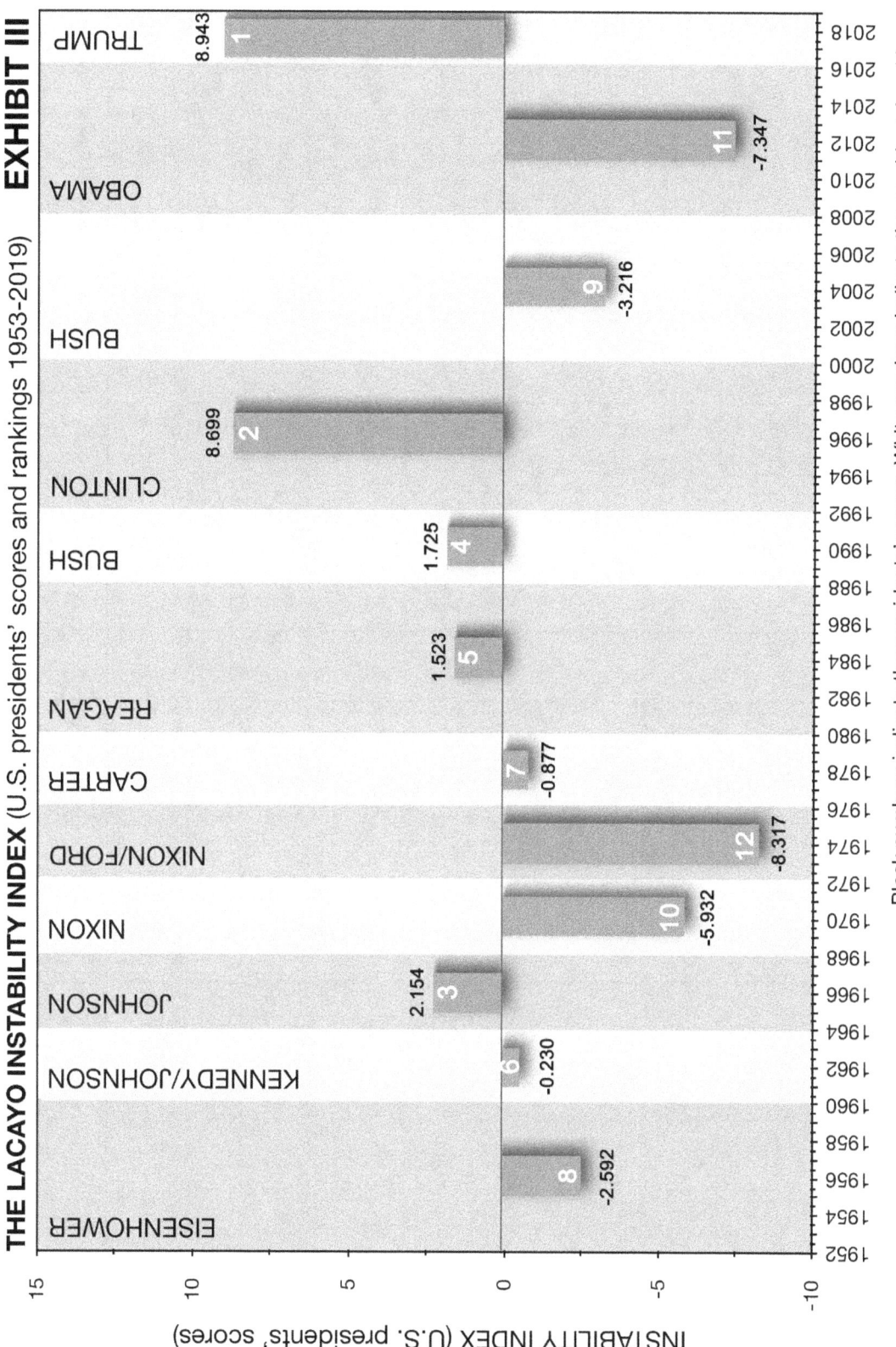

EXHIBIT III

THE LACAYO INSTABILITY INDEX (U.S. presidents' scores and rankings 1953-2019)

INSTABILITY INDEX (U.S. presidents' scores)

President	Score	Rank
TRUMP	8.943	1
OBAMA	-7.347	11
BUSH	-3.216	9
CLINTON	8.699	2
BUSH	1.725	4
REAGAN	1.523	5
CARTER	-0.877	7
NIXON/FORD	-8.317	12
NIXON	-5.932	10
JOHNSON	2.154	3
KENNEDY/JOHNSON	-0.230	6
EISENHOWER	-2.592	8

Black numbers indicate the presidents' scores. White numbers indicate the presidents' rankings.

23